FLOWERS FROM SHAKESPEARE'S GARDEN :

Pictured by Walter Crane

Cassell & Compy. Ltd.

Flowers from
Shakespeare's
Garden

To the Countess of Warwick,
whose delightful Old English
Garden at Easton Lodge sug-
gested this book of fancies, it is
now inscribed.

FLOWERS FROM SHAKESPEARE'S GARDEN:
a Posy from the Plays, pictured by Walter Crane

Cassell & Co: Ltd ❧ 1909 ❧

'O, PROSERPINA,
For the flowers now, that, frighted, thou lett'st fall
From Dis's wagon!

That come before the swallow dares, and take daffodils,[3.]
The winds of March with beauty;

1786

violets, dim

But sweeter than the lids of Juno's eyes

Or Cytherea's breath;

"   pale primroses,
That die unmarried, ere they can behold
Bright Phœbus in his strength, a malady
Most incident to maids;

bold oxlips, and

The crown- -imperial;

lilies of all kinds,

The flower-de-luce being one...!"

"

—Here's flowers for you;

"Hot lavender,

mints,

savorie, marjoram ;

The marigold that goes to bed with the sun,
And with him rises weeping;

Perdita.
Winter's Tale
Act: IV. Sc. III.

"The fairest flowers o' the season

Are our carnations, "

Perdita.
Winter's Tale
Act. IV. Sc. III.

She went to the garden for parsley

(Taming of the Shrew
Act: IV. Sc: 4.)

"Their lips were four red roses on a stalk,
Which in their summer beauty kissed each other"

Richard III., Act iv, Sc. 3

"*Enter* OPHELIA, *fantastically dressed with straws and flowers.*"

"There's rosemary,
　　　　that's for remembrance;

— and there is pansies,
  that's for thoughts."

"There's fennel for you,

and columbines:

— there's rue for you; and here's some for me:
—we may call it, herb-grace o' Sundays:—

—There's a daisy:—

Hamlet. Act. IV. Sc. VI.

"I know a bank where the
wild thyme blows, —

Quite over-canopied with luscious
woodbine.

"With sweet
        musk roses,

and with
eglantine."

Midsummer Night's
Dream, Act ii., sc. 1

"CERES, most bounteous lady, thy rich lees
Of wheat, rye, barley,"

30.

Tempest, Act iv, Sc.1,

"Allons! allons! sowed cockle reap'd no corn."

Love's Labour's Lost, Act Iv.
Sc. 3.

"The azured harebell, like thy veins."

Cymbeline, Act iv, Sc. 2.

" Larksheels trim "

Two Noble Kinsmen.

" Get you some of this distilled Carduus Benedictus [34.]
and lay it to your heart; —
" Why Benedictus? You have some moral in this
Benedictus
" Moral? No, by my
troth. I have no
moral meaning;
I meant, plain
Holy thistle "

Much Ado
about Nothing.
Act III., Sc. 4.

"The female ivy so
Enrings the barky fingers of the elm"

Midsummer Night's Dream.
Act V., Sc. 2

"The strawberry grows underneath the nettle,
And wholesome berries thrive and ripen best
Neighboured by   fruit of baser   quality"

Henry V.,
Act I., Sc. I.

"Gives not the hawthorne-bush a sweeter shade
To shepherds, looking on their silly sheep,
Than doth a rich embroidered canopy
To kings that fear their subjects' treachery?"
3 Henry VI., Act ii., sc. 5.

"If reasons were as plentiful as blackberries"

1 Henry IV., Act ii., Sc. 4

"Heigh-ho! sing heigh-ho! unto the green holly"

As You Like
It,
Act ii., Sc 7.

'Prerogative of age, crowns, sceptres, laurels.'

Troilus & Cressida, Act i., Sc., 3

Finis

CASSELL & COMPANY, LIMITED, LATE LONDON.

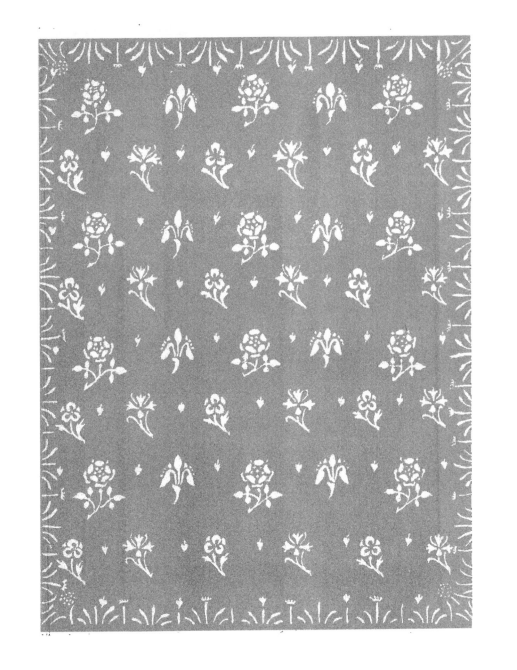

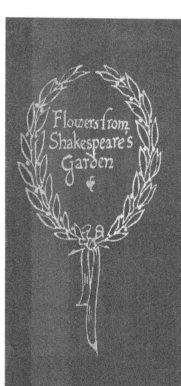

Flowers from Shakespeare's Garden

Cassell & Co: Ltd

Milton Keynes UK
Ingram Content Group UK Ltd.
UKHW022025110923
428497UK00005B/102